The Promise and Perils of Technology™

VIRTUAL REALITY AND YOU

Jeff Mapua

Rosen YA
New York

Published in 2020 by The Rosen Publishing Group, Inc.
29 East 21st Street, New York, NY 10010

Copyright © 2020 by The Rosen Publishing Group, Inc.

First Edition

All rights reserved. No part of this book may be reproduced in any form without permission in writing from the publisher, except by a reviewer.

Library of Congress Cataloging-in-Publication Data

Names: Mapua, Jeff, author.
Title: Virtual reality and you / Jeff Mapua.
Description: New York: Rosen Publishing, 2020. | Series: The promise and perils of technology | Includes bibliographical references and index. | Audience: Grades 7 to 12.
Identifiers: LCCN 2018046287| ISBN 9781508188377 (library bound) | ISBN 9781508188360 (pbk.)
Subjects. LCSH: Virtual reality—Juvenile literature.
Classification: LCC QA76.9.V5 M35 2020 | DDC 006.8—dc23
LC record available at https://lccn.loc.gov/2018046287

Manufactured in the United States of America

CONTENTS

	Introduction	4
1	Virtually Reality	7
2	Dangers of VR	15
3	The First Wave	22
4	Reality Reborn	30
5	In the Real World	37
6	The Future	43
	Glossary	51
	For More Information	53
	For Further Reading	55
	Bibliography	56
	Index	62

INTRODUCTION

A student walks along the Motoyasu River, a branch of the Ota River, in southwestern Japan and looks around at the buildings. Suddenly, flying overhead, a single plane comes into view. A sudden flash of light is followed by a tremendous explosion. The student is witnessing the history-changing atomic bombing of Hiroshima by the United States on August 6, 1945. The student, however, is actually safe and sound in a classroom—not in the year 1945, but in 2018. Through the magic of virtual reality (VR), she and others can learn about that horrific event in World War II history by experiencing it in an artificial, three-dimensional (3D) environment.

Virtual reality is a technology that allows people to view or interact with a simulated environment. A simulated environment is one that is created in a machine such as a computer or mobile phone. With the use of specially designed goggles or eyewear, people can look around in environments that computer programmers have created. VR can even stimulate other senses besides sight such as hearing, smell, or touch. Some people say that the experience is like being taken to a new world.

For students at a technical high school in Fukuyama, located about 52 miles (84 kilometers) east from Hiroshima, VR enables the students to have a history lesson they may never forget. According to an August 2018 article in *Newsweek*, the 1945 atomic blast killed nearly eighty thousand people in Hiroshima within the first hour.

Introduction

Fukuyama Technical High School student Namio Matsura wears a VR headset and looks around a virtual environment recreating a major moment in history.

Virtual Reality and You

Eighteen-year-old Yuhi Nakagawa, one of the Fukuyama students who worked on the VR project, said at first that he did not have much interest in the bombing of Hiroshima and avoided the topic. Virtual reality allows anyone to see and experience this historic event from a different perspective. That approach was the goal that these high school students aimed for when they created the virtual reality simulation of the moments before, during, and after the Hiroshima bombing. Their aspiration is to make certain that this kind of tragic event never occurs again.

The students also recreated the sights and sounds for Hiroshima survivors who are today reaching advanced ages. Katsushi Hasegawa is a computer teacher who supervised the computation skill research club that was responsible for creating the five-minute VR experience. Hasegawa said, "Those who knew the city very well tell us it's done very well. They say it's very nostalgic."

Virtual reality technology has been in the making for decades. Only in the latter part of the twentieth century did the technology catch up with people's imaginations. Some critics say that virtual reality poses dangers to those who use it. They believe VR can hurt people's eyes and brains. Others are worried about users' privacy and their becoming less sensitive to violence in the real world. With the lack of long-term research into the technology, they may be right to fear VR. But people will continue to innovate with VR. Medical students can peer into virtual bodies and view internal body systems in ways that are impossible in the real world. VR therapy can lead some people who have been diagnosed with certain fears to overcome them. Gamers can view alien worlds from the eyes of their favorite characters. The possibilities of VR are endless.

CHAPTER 1

Virtually Reality

Imagine visiting a new world where anything is possible. The rules of reality are regularly bent or broken. People can fly, the grass is blue, and the sky is filled with alien spaceships. VR, a technology with immense potential, can create any type of experience you can dream up.

What Is Virtual Reality?

Sometimes a person watches a movie and loses himself or herself in the story, characters, and plot. This total absorption is considered an immersive experience. Other immersive experiences can come from different types of media. People can get lost within the music they are listening to, for example. VR is an immersive technological experience. It is an artificial environment experienced through sights provided by a computer. Someone using a virtual reality headset is called a user. VR involves displaying 3D images that appear to surround the user.

Whatever worlds people can imagine, those can be created in the virtual world. Users can soar through skies like a bird or explore a sunken ship deep below the surface of the ocean. People have been dreaming of VR technology for decades because of the endless experiences that might be possible with it.

Today, virtual reality is achieved through computer technology. There are two basic parts to VR. One part is worn over a user's eyes. This device comes in many forms such as specially designed

Virtual Reality and You

Virtual reality is an immersive technology with applications in gaming, medicine, education, and more.

eyeglasses, a viewfinder, or a headset. Attached to the headset is a small screen, similar to a computer monitor. The screen displays images that the user views through special lenses. These lenses help magnify whatever is onscreen. Generally speaking, it is like looking at a computer screen inches away while wearing magnifying glasses over each eye.

Some headsets, or head-mounted displays, feature one screen while others have two. A popular style of virtual reality uses a mobile phone as a screen. The mobile phone is placed inside a special viewfinder or headset that is equipped with lenses to magnify the screen.

Virtually Reality

The second part of a VR setup powers the headset. The more immersive virtual reality setups today are run by computers. The computer runs the software that calculates what to show on the screen. Many programmers create games that transport users to other imagined worlds. Others create computer versions of places where people can gather and interact, such as a rec room. Some forms of VR use mobile phones to run a headset. Mobile phones are placed inside a headset and run VR-enabled applications. These apps could be games, video players, internet browsers, and more.

With the headset on, a user can look up, down, and spin around to see what's behind him or her. This capability is particularly effective

Degrees of Freedom

In the mid-2010s, VR devices could be separated into two types. These are three degrees of freedom (3DOF) and six degrees of freedom (6DOF). Both types refer to how users can move in their virtual environments.

A 3DOF headset allows users to look up and down, left and right, and spin around in a circle. Objects remain the same distance from a user. A 6DOF headset enables users to move just as they do in the real world. They can look in any direction, and move toward, away from, and around virtual objects.

The computing component of a VR system must be able to track how the user moves in the real world. Some systems use cameras placed around a room that tell the computer where the user is within a set area. Other systems use cameras placed on the headset that look out into the real world. This technology, called inside-out tracking, creates a map of a user's real environment. Users have found that 6DOF provides a great sense of immersion in the virtual world.

Virtual Reality and You

In 2018, improved virtual reality experiences required users to connect their headsets to a separate computer with advanced graphical capabilities, among other requirements.

Virtually Reality

in scary games that are so frightening people rip off their headset out of fear!

Immersion

Although being able to look around a virtual environment can be entertaining, true immersion requires interaction. This step means that a user should be able to pick up and hold items within the virtual world. Today, VR systems are provided with controllers that become a user's virtual hands. The technology makes a user feel like they are truly inside the virtual world. Some companies have even designed wireless controllers that are worn like a glove to improve immersion. Sensors on the gloves mimic hand and finger gestures, such as when a user wiggles his or her fingers or grabs an object.

Sound is another important factor in making users feel like they are really in the virtual world. New technology today has introduced directional hearing that makes sound feel like it is coming from a specific location within the VR environment.

Other additions have been introduced to VR. These include ways to recreate smells so a virtual garden will produce flower scents. Technology has been introduced to send electronic pulses to a user's hands so it will feel like that person is holding whatever item he or she picks up in the virtual world. There are many applications for this technology. People will feel like they are really holding a

11

Virtual Reality and You

virtual item in their hands. Two people could even "hold hands" in the virtual world and feel like the other person is with him or her no matter how far apart they really are.

Benefits of VR

Virtual reality can help people in many ways beyond entertainment. Applications including Virtual Orator, Speech Center VR, and Public Speaking VR aim to help people overcome their fear of public speaking. Additional applications address other disorders such

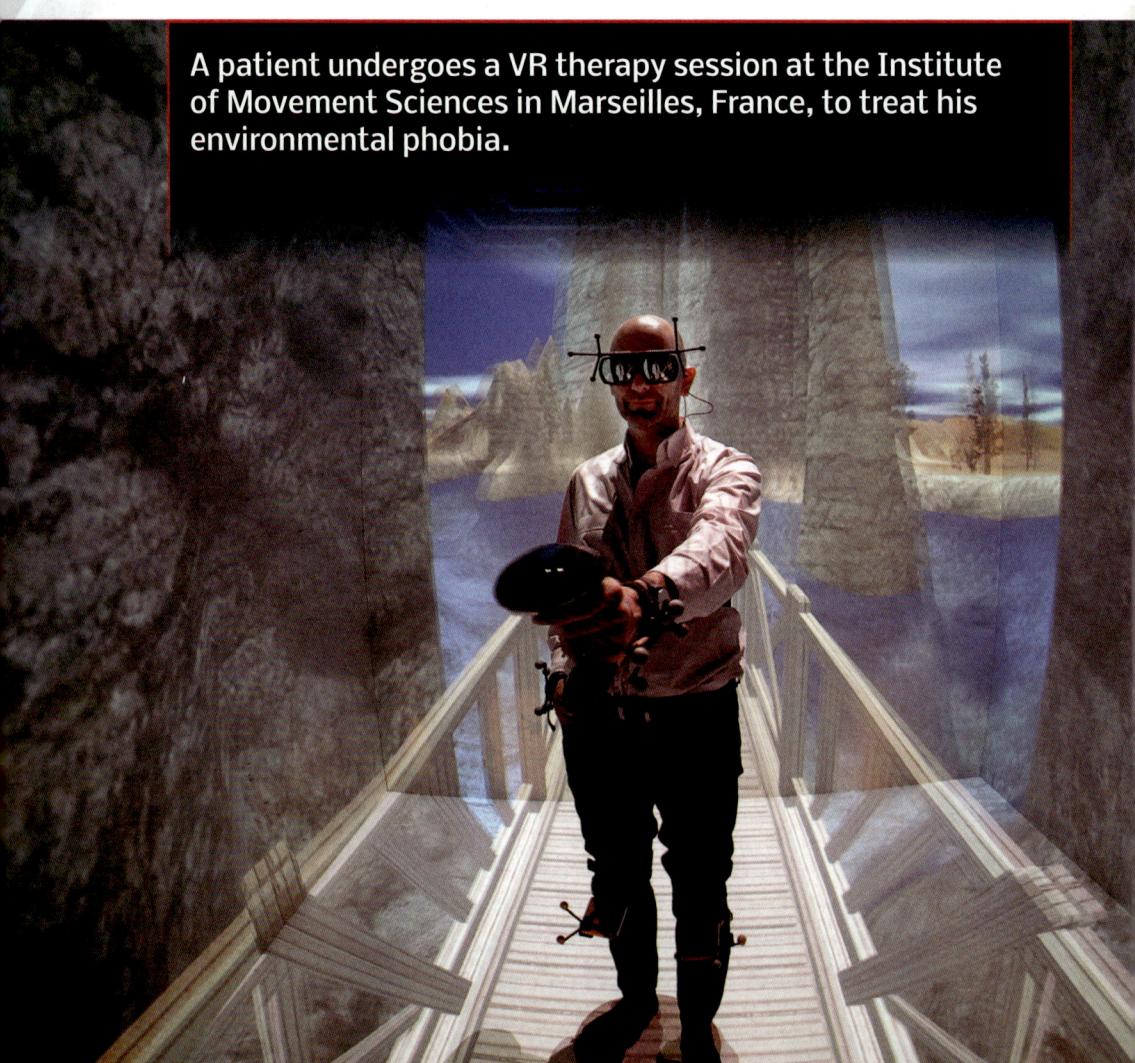

A patient undergoes a VR therapy session at the Institute of Movement Sciences in Marseilles, France, to treat his environmental phobia.

as post-traumatic stress, eating, anxiety, and smoking addiction. Therapy for anxiety-related and eating disorders have already been tested on real patients.

The Department of Psychology at the University of Oxford in England used software called Now I Can Do Heights in their tests. The program used immersive virtual reality therapy to treat people who had been diagnosed with a fear of heights. Test subjects had six, thirty-minute sessions over the course of two weeks. They wore VR headsets and were exposed to varying heights in a ten-story office complex, such as riding a moving platform into the open space of the complex's atrium or trying to rescue a cat from a tree. The researchers found that VR exposure therapy was successful in many of their test subjects. There was a 68 percent average reduction in the fear of heights that lasted more than a year. This result was better than that from traditional treatment with a therapist.

Teachers are also looking to take advantage of VR technology. There is interest in many educational fields, including engineering, architecture, nursing, and design, in using VR as teaching and training aids. One interesting idea was to create crime scenes for teaching students in law enforcement. Criminology students could walk around a scene to see if they could find clues to help solve the crime. Medical students also used VR to learn human anatomy. Several of those who participated in VR learning claimed that the visualization helped them better understand the concepts they were studying.

Augmented Reality

Similar to virtual reality, augmented reality adds a new dimension to users' lives. Virtual reality transports people to different simulated environments. Augmented reality (AR) enhances people's real-world environments.

Virtual Reality and You

Augmented reality devices have similar components to VR. There is a headset paired with a machine to handle the computing. At first, AR was just computer-generated images superimposed over the real world. Over time, AR began to include interactions with the computer-generated images users saw. Many use the terms "mixed reality" and "augmented reality" to describe the same experience.

One popular form of AR occurs during US football games. In 1998, a company called Sportvision added a new feature to television broadcasts of football games. Sportvision's goal was to help viewers understand what point on the field a football team needed to reach to get a first down. They created AR technology that placed a yellow line on the field to mark it. The line was invisible to players on the real field, of course. To viewers at home, however, they witnessed an augmented, or enhanced, reality. Today the Sportvision technology in football TV broadcasts also includes distance arrows and yard lines that are covered by snow, among other enhancements.

CHAPTER 2

Dangers of VR

Virtual reality critics believe that there are risks of physical ailments as a result of using a VR system. Researchers are looking into the possible harm done to young people's brains, for instance. The experiences may be virtual, but the physical dangers are very real.

Tangled Up

Virtual reality headset designers eventually want users to require only a head-mounted display to enter a virtual world and not be connected to a computer or mobile phone. This concept is illustrated in various headsets that were released in 2018 and that are considered as standalone. A standalone headset means that the entire VR system is contained within a headset. Until these standalone devices include advanced computing components, virtual reality must still rely on computers to create believable immersion. In the meantime, the headset must be connected to a computer with wires. The wires pass information and data between the headset and computer. Wireless solutions for headsets were introduced in 2016 and 2017, but at an additional cost to users.

In effect, users carry a wire around a room as they interact with their virtual environments. The danger is that users can get tangled up within these wires. Because the user is blind to the real world while wearing a headset, the dangling wires pose a physical danger. People have invented ingenious solutions to this problem. These

Virtual Reality and You

While users are exploring virtual worlds, they must remain aware of obstacles in the real world, such as wires and furniture, that can cause serious injury.

include complicated rigs attached to a ceiling that keep wires from getting tangled in a user's feet. At tech demos, headset companies have been known to follow testers around, carefully moving the wires out of harm's way.

Headsets are basically blindfolds. Users can accidentally run into real walls while roaming an open virtual area. Controllers

Dangers of VR

also introduce the danger of breaking real-world fixtures. There are many stories of VR users wildly waving their controllers around and accidentally breaking lamps, television sets, or the controllers themselves.

Nausea

A common side effect of VR is nausea or motion sickness. Some users report discomfort while engaged in a VR application. People have been known to become too dizzy to continue with a VR session. The advancement of technology has helped a bit to reduce motion

VR Death

One tragic example of the physical dangers of VR happened to a man in Russia. In 2017, a forty-four-year old man was found dead in his apartment. Police determined that the man wore VR goggles when he slipped. He fell on a glass table that broke into shards. He suffered cuts from the broken glass and then bled to death.

This accident illustrates the dangers of moving around in a virtual environment while being cut off from the real one. Users may become so immersed in their VR world that they forget that there are still real obstacles, such as tables and walls in their way.

VR headset manufacturer HTC warns users that they are blind to the world around them while wearing the HTC headset. The best way to avoid injury is to have someone watch the user. Users should also clear the area of anything that could become an obstruction or hazard or use an area free from perilous objects. These dangers can include unattended pets and children, furniture, and ceiling fans.

Virtual Reality and You

sickness in virtual reality. However, motion sickness was still an issue years after systems such as the HTC Vive and Oculus Rift were first released in 2016.

Some people experience nausea because of slow-moving games. This circumstance is true particularly for games and applications that rely on controllers for users to move around. For example, instead of walking around to explore a virtual environment, people use a joystick to control their movements. At the same time, users can turn their heads to look around. This disconnect, when using controllers to move while turning their heads to observe, causes motion sickness.

Simulated motion has been known to cause a disorder called simulator sickness. The phenomenon has been discovered in flight simulations over the years. The condition could be the result of the

Companies such as HTC have introduced handheld controllers to improve immersion and relieve the nausea some people experience with virtual reality.

neurological effects of VR movement. Technology is a suspect for causing these effects. Frame rate describes how fast or frequent new frames are displayed on a screen. A lower frequency rate has been found to cause more nausea. In addition, if a user's virtual body does not move in sync with the person's real body, the situation can cause a disconnect in that individual's brain. This disconnect can cause motion sickness.

Sometimes nausea also occurs when the head-mounted display does not properly fit an individual. A person's eyes have a hard time focusing with the lenses. The eye strain can cause nausea, too.

The common recommendation to fight motion sickness is for users to take frequent breaks from VR. VR software designers have also tried different tricks to help users who have nausea. These include giving a user a visible nose in the software and virtual hands.

Too Close

Virtual reality headsets need a screen to be held inches from users' faces, only to be magnified even further with lenses. Most health care professionals frown on keeping a display inches from one's face for hours at a time because of the possibility of damaging one's eyesight.

However, according to a 2017 article published by the American Academy of Ophthalmology, which specializes in eye health, VR technology does not pose a threat to eye development, health, or function. Pediatric ophthalmologist Dr. Stephen Lipsky, who is quoted in the article, says, "Age limitations for VR technology might make sense for content, but as far as we know this technology poses no threat to the eyes." Still, the recommendation is to take breaks to avoid eye strain or fatigue. People blink less when using a digital screen device compared to other times. They also suggest that people who wear eyeglasses should continue wearing them while wearing a VR headset.

Virtual Reality and You

Cognitive Issues

Although eye health is not a major concern for VR users, other health risks are, especially for young people. According to Robin McKie's article in the *Guardian*, scientists based at Leeds University in England believe "continued use of VR sets could trigger eyesight and balance problems in young people."

The long-term effects of virtual reality are an unknown. Although safety warnings don't recommend prolonged use, there is still much to learn about VR's effect on growing brains.

Dangers of VR

The researchers ran tests on children, from ages eight to twelve, using VR. They found that eyesight was not negatively affected in major ways. But researchers did find that the ability to detect differences in distances was. The children's balance was thrown off once they took off their headsets. They recommended that changes be made to the VR devices so that possible physiological damage to children could be averted. The scientists also call for more research into the field to determine what risks VR poses to developing brains.

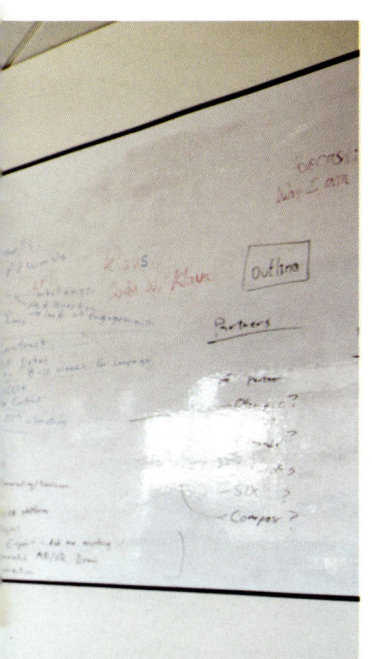

The study is one of the first to look closely at VR technology because long-term effects on children are unknown. As reported by Sandee LaMotte for CNN, most studies on the health effects of VR on children have involved young adults, not younger children. The technology has not been around long enough to know how it can affect children over time. VR is still a young industry.

CHAPTER 3

The First Wave

Health hazards are an issue that creators of virtual reality technology have to address more fully. However, there was a time when early developers thought virtual reality might not even be a possibility because of the technological shortcomings.

Computer Revolution

Machines called digital computers were used in the 1930s and early 1940s. Early mainframe computers, such as the 1965 RCA Spectra 70 series, were expensive to use and maintain, according to an online article by the Computer History Museum. In 1972, the HP 3000 computer cost an incredible $95,000, as reported by Evan Comen in *USA Today*. Comen also wrote that by 1976, the Apple I cost $667, making personal computers a reality for home use. It was around the mid-1980s that the first attempts at creating virtual worlds came to life. The National Aeronautics and Space Administration (NASA) created some of the earliest virtual reality technology along with a few universities that were VR pioneers during the 1980s. NASA's technology involved large goggles, a headset with headphones and a microphone, and a glove—all wired to a computer.

In 1962, Morton Heilig created a motorcycle ride simulator called Sensorama. On Sensorama's display, viewers watched a short film about a fixed route through New York while having their other senses besides sight stimulated. The "ride" included sound, scents, and vibration. People could not interact with the short movie, though.

The First Wave

NASA's early VR technology was known as Virtual Interface Environment Workstation (VIEW) and included gloves fitted with sensors to create virtual hands.

Virtual Reality and You

In 1968, computer graphic pioneer Ivan Sutherland designed a head-mounted display. His idea was to find a way to track the user's movements and correctly display graphics based on where the user was looking. He even wrote about his desire to include smell and taste in his system. It would be years, however, before advancements in technology would make his ideas a possibility.

In 1982, flight simulators were a huge step forward for virtual reality technology. Much of the technology was worked on at the United States Air Force's Armstrong Medical Research Laboratory. This technology was aimed to help train fighter pilots. The simulators took pilots through various scenarios and tested actions such as friend-or-foe identification and targeting, threat, or flight path information. The research uncovered challenges to create realistic VR such as fast display update rates or frame rates, short lag time between real-world and virtual-world movement, realistic shadows and textures, and techniques to manage the display of complex worlds. Although the air force was able to create realistic VR, it came at a cost of millions of dollars for each simulator.

NASA then stepped into the VR world in 1984 with Virtual Visual Environment Display, or VIVED. Intended for training astronauts, the system had many of the components of modern VR systems. It featured a glove, called DataGlove, that users wore and a head-mounted display called the EyePhone.

Over time computer systems could handle the actions that were needed for virtual reality to work. These actions included animating images and sound at the same time as a computer receives data, a feature called real-time. People created new ways to enter data into and receive data from a computer, and they gave computers the capability to handle additional power, too.

The First Wave

Gaming Pushes Forward

Video games became a major economic force beginning with the Nintendo Entertainment System (NES), which was manufactured by Nintendo Company, in the mid-1980s. The company helped increase interest in virtual reality with innovations such as their Power Glove, released in 1989. The Power Glove was a controller for the NES that players wore on their hand. The gray, forearm-length glove had a black sensor resting on the back of the hand, while a control pad with numerous buttons was attached to the forearm.

With hand gestures, players moved characters on the screen. The Power Glove had ultrasonic transmitters that connected to three receivers people had to set up around their televisions. After the long set-up process, people could then experience a version of virtual reality.

The Power Glove Lends a Hand

Although the Power Glove was a failure for Nintendo, people found other uses for the device. One musician programmed the glove to control instruments on his computer. An animator uses the Power Glove to help create stop-motion animations. The enhanced glove uses Bluetooth technology to communicate with animation software.

Nineteen-year-old Easton LaChappelle used the sensors from the Power Glove to help another person out in a major way. The sensors convert real hand movements into robotic motion. With the technology, he built a low-cost robot arm that could be controlled by thoughts. The robot arm can be used to help people who have lost use of their arms and hands.

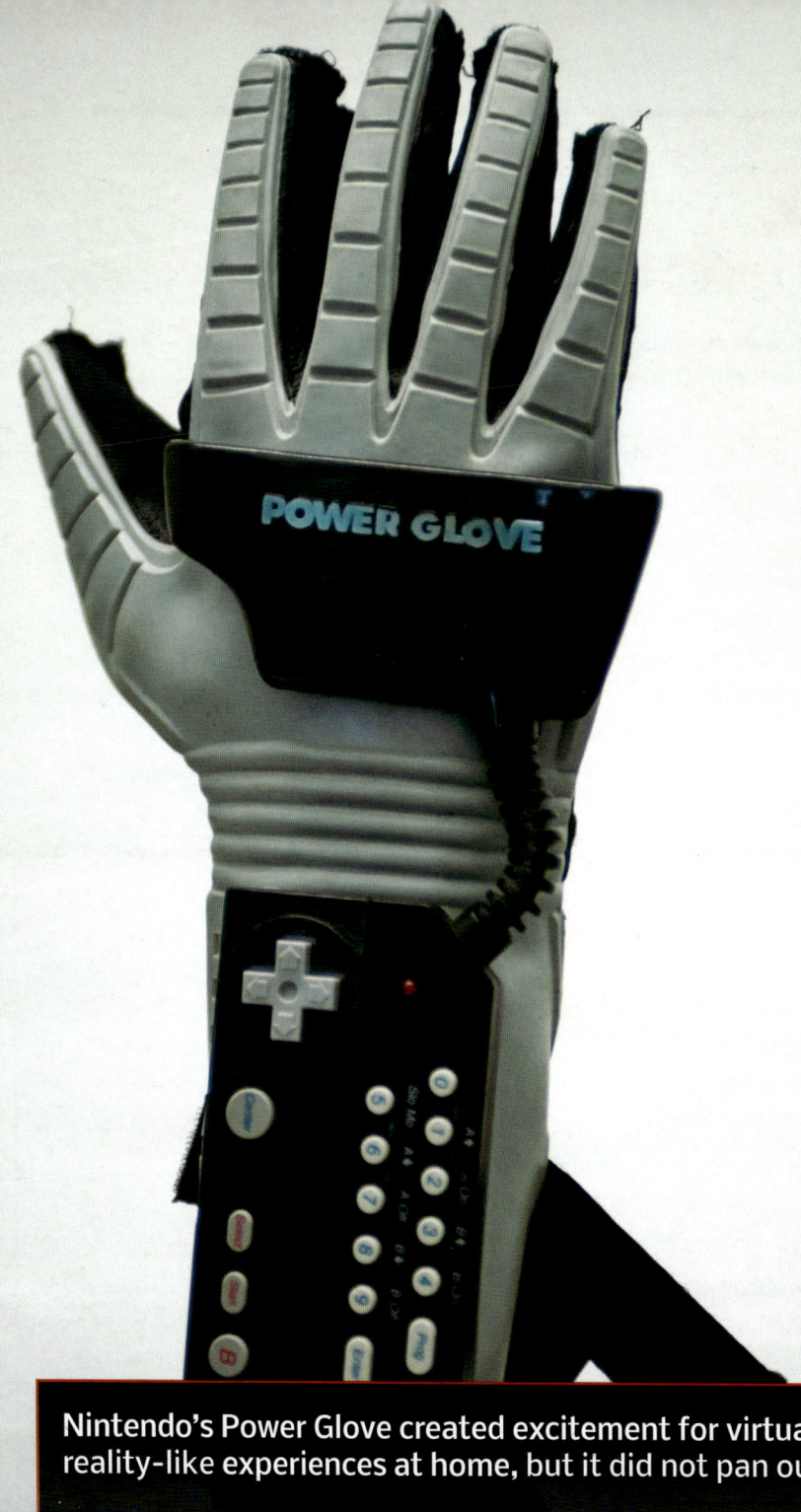

Nintendo's Power Glove created excitement for virtual reality-like experiences at home, but it did not pan out.

The First Wave

The advertising campaign for the Power Glove created high levels of excitement. However, people quickly discovered that the technology did not deliver on its promise—the finger motions were confusing to work and didn't function all the time. The Power Glove ended up as a massive failure for Nintendo.

Harsh Reality of VR Technology

The first attempts at VR faced many technological challenges. Eventually these challenges doomed the first wave in making VR popular.

Virtuality

A British company named Virtuality created a virtual reality system that played a handful of games. The system included a headset, controllers, and a special platform that kept users in a small, enclosed space. Each machine cost $78,000. At first, Virtuality sold its equipment to companies looking to use the VR systems in their businesses. For example, oil companies used the machines to train workers on escape drills, and the auto companies Ford and Kawasaki designed test driving simulations for their test drivers to test vehicles.

Virtuality wanted people to buy the machines for home use. They introduced the machines to video game arcades where people could pay five dollars for a few minutes' worth of playing time. An incredible amount of hype followed the company and its machines. However, that publicity did not last.

VR depended on immersive experiences, and it took only a few moments for people to realize that Virtuality's systems did not deliver these experiences. The high-profile failure of Virtuality was a massive blow to consumer interest in VR.

Virtual Reality and You

Virtual Boy

Nintendo did not give up the virtual reality dream with the failure of the Power Glove. In 1994, the video game company released the Virtual Boy. It was a stationary headset that players looked into. Nevertheless, it also proved to be a failure for Nintendo. Players did not like the lack of head tracking. While using the headset, players could look in only one direction. Also, its screen was displayed only in red because of the headset's poor technology.

Moore's Law is a law of computing technology. It states that the number of transistors on a chip doubles about every two years. This law means that computers are twice as powerful today as they were just two years previously. Virtual reality in the 1990s was far ahead of VR in the 1960s, of course. However, VR was not yet ready for mainstream use.

Concerns Are Raised

In 1996, TV anchor Brian Williams of NBC News and correspondent Kerry Sanders aired a **report on VR and simulator sickness in a Focus** segment, and asked, "What happens when you go from that virtual world

Nintendo followed the Power Glove with the Virtual Boy, another failed attempt at bringing VR to consumers.

The First Wave

and back to the real world and drive a car?" The report featured researchers from the University of Central Florida, who found VR exposure could result in dizziness, nausea, and loss of coordination. Psychologist Robert Kennedy compared the effects of VR to drinking too much alcohol.

In his report, Sanders includes a few tips from researchers on how one can avoid these side effects. The researchers suggest simply stopping the use of VR equipment to take frequent breaks. Researchers also suggest that the price of VR equipment and accessories will help minimize the number of people who are affected by VR use. Because the technology is so expensive, many people will choose not to use a VR machine at an arcade or purchase a system for their homes.

Early VR was too expensive for most people, and the immersion experience was disappointing for many. These failed attempts ended the first wave of interest in VR technology. It would take a few rounds of Moore's Law before VR could make its comeback.

CHAPTER 4

Reality Reborn

Excitement for the promise of virtual reality began to run high following advances in technology and renewed interest from companies. But did this mean that virtual reality as a technological industry had finally caught on?

Advances in Technology

Over time, technology companies developed computers that were faster and more powerful than earlier inventions. Many smartphones of 2018 are more powerful than computers from the 1980s. Computers improved in many different ways. Computers in the second decade of the 2000s store much more data than those from the 1990s. In the 1990s, a device called a floppy disk saved data on a magnetic strip inside a piece of plastic. Floppy disks were able to hold up to 1.4 megabytes of data. For reference, this amount is not enough space to save most mp3 music files. Eventually, technology companies invented portable storage devices called USB flash drives. Flash drives store the equivalent amount of data as 22,222 floppy disks. As of 2018, computers can store three million times the amount of data that one floppy disk stores.

Computer manufacturers made computer screens more powerful as well. In 2018, all television screens and computer monitors produce high-definition images. These images are clearer and crisper than the best TV that was available in the 1990s. Early high-definition screens displayed about 300,000 pixels. That number has increased to

Reality Reborn

more than two million pixels, which means that smaller details can be observed today. These advances are good news for virtual reality.

Oculus Rift

Mobile phone technology improved to the point that people began using their smartphones for virtual reality. They took advantage of the crisp displays and computing power that was supplied in touchscreen phones. Although these headsets, such as the Google Cardboard, were great first steps, they were not complete experiences. The Oculus Rift, however, aimed to be just that.

Oculus Rift began as a project in April 2012 by nineteen-year-old Palmer Luckey. His idea was simple. He placed a small screen inside a headset. He then sold do-it-yourself kits online so others could

Palmer Luckey helped popularize the wave of virtual reality in the mid-2010s with his homegrown Oculus technology.

Virtual Reality and You

make their own VR systems. Luckey's work was noticed by influential people in the video game industry. Oculus Rift eventually became a million-dollar company. Then Facebook bought the company for $2 billion in 2014.

The Oculus Rift works by connecting a headset to a computer with fast processing speed and a high-end video card to display high-quality graphics. Users can control their movements with a video game controller or with optional handheld controllers that mimic hand and finger gestures. Two sensors are set up around a room or area to capture the user's movements and translate them into a virtual environment. A third sensor is optional for improved tracking and six degrees of freedom.

One of the biggest obstacles for users is the required computer to run the headset. The headset itself originally cost $599 in 2016. People interested in an Oculus Rift would also have to purchase a powerful computer that could cost more than $500 itself. Always check the manufacturer's requirements regarding the computer's graphics and video card, central processing unit (CPU), memory, video output, and operating system to ensure that the computer can accommodate the headset. Both Oculus Rift and Vive have applications that check for computer compatibility. This powerful computer stipulation also means that the headset must always be connected to the computer via wires.

The screens inside the headset, although powerful, are not capable of displaying completely realistic graphics. Finally, users' reviews of the Oculus Rift have mentioned that nausea is still a significant side effect.

HTC Vive

A challenger to the Oculus Rift, HTC's Vive headset, beat the competition to market. The Vive was the first high-end virtual reality device available for purchase. In 2014, Valve teamed up with HTC, a Taiwanese technology company known for its smartphones. Together

Reality Reborn

they released the HTC Vive in April 2016. Working in a similar way as the Oculus Rift, the Vive requires two tracking base stations positioned around a room or area for six degrees of freedom. Users control their hand movements with a controller for each hand.

Vive users have to be aware of the wires connecting the headset to the computer. Not doing so can cause serious injury or, occasionally,

The HTC Vive headset utilized two cameras to track a user's movements and translate them into a virtual environment.

even death. The price is also a barrier to entry. Not only is a high-end computer required, but the Vive originally cost $799 in 2016. Some users complain about motion sickness from the system, too. This condition could be because of the screen quality, which has what is known as the screen-door effect. This result describes the Vive's displays, which, when seen through the headset's lenses, make it look like a screen door is overlaying the entire field of view.

Microsoft

Microsoft's October 2017 entry into VR was another headset that required a computer to which it would connect. Called Mixed Reality headsets, they suffered from the same roadblocks as the Rift and Vive headsets. However, Microsoft's headsets were made by various companies and sold at more affordable prices, such as a version priced at $400.

The Microsoft system also did not require external sensors to track users' movements. Instead, it relied on cameras located on the headset to keep track of movement and the controllers. This type of tracking is known as inside out because the cameras looked "out" at the world as opposed to cameras looking "in" toward the headset. Although wireless, the experience is not as immersive as external tracking.

Where Is Everybody?

The second wave of VR enthusiasm was a roller coaster of activity. The *New York Times* predicted a "virtual reality revolution" in 2015. Only two years later did the online technology news publisher TechCrunch declare that "This VR Cycle Is Dead." According to

Reality Reborn

Acer's Mixed Reality headset was one of several Microsoft-powered VR headsets launched in 2017 that did not require external cameras to track user movement.

Virtual Reality and You

PlayStation VR

Sony, makers of the PlayStation video game console, made a headset that did not require a computer. The company introduced PlayStation VR, an add-on to their popular console. The VR system was initially available for $399 in October 2016, and it required only a PlayStation 4 to run. It uses a single external camera to track a player's movements and two handheld controllers.

Although the entire system was more affordable than the pricier computer systems such as the Rift and Vive, it was also not as immersive. Reviews mentioned loss of tracking issues, particularly with the controllers. Although the headset was said to be less comfortable than others, Sony was more successful in getting content made for its system. Sony sold many units and early reports are that there will be an improved version available in 2020 or 2021.

many analysts, the number one challenge for widespread acceptance of VR is the lack of engaging content. People who own one of the available headsets find that there is not as much to do with them and VR as they had hoped.

Despite the excitement, application and software developers are cautiously testing the virtual reality market. An anonymous video game developer told TechCrunch, "It feels like the second-wave bubble of VR is about to burst. The technology is incredibly exciting, and it has the potential to be huge one day. Unfortunately neither the hardware nor the software is ready for that yet."

CHAPTER 5

In the Real World

Virtual reality is more than headsets and computers. Its popularity extends to various movies and books about virtual worlds. Businesses and educators were interested in using VR despite the challenges for the VR industry to overcome.

The Shaky Business of VR

Major companies such as Facebook, Google, and Microsoft have rushed to set the standards of VR. This push is despite the point that virtual reality is failing to become mainstream technology. The industry's growth since VR was reintroduced in 2013 has been slow. The headsets that are available each have their own drawbacks including price, difficulty of setup, and lack of content.

At the 2018 Consumer Electronics Show, technology companies announced new VR products and goals. Google revealed its new Mirage Solo headset, made with a partner company, Lenovo. This headset would not require a powerful computer and would still provide 6DOF experiences.

Meanwhile, HTC announced its updated version of the Vive headset. The headset would have better lenses for clearer images and improved graphics. Facebook, on the other hand, detailed its own low-priced headset that would not require a computer or a mobile device. This headset would cost only $200, and provide users with 3DOF experiences.

Virtual Reality and You

According to Mark Gurman in a March 2018 article on Bloomberg.com, the Consumer Technology Association predicted that VR would grow by 25 percent in 2018. Some people in the VR industry believe that enthusiasm and a positive outlook for VR have been helped by the release of the 2018 movie *Ready Player One*. Although rumors of Amazon looking to release their own VR headset were not confirmed at the show, Gurman reported that Apple was pursuing augmented reality technology.

To help with sales, the VR industry has come up with different ways to get the technology in people's hands. One strategy is to integrate VR with education.

Ready Player One

In 2018, Ernest Cline's novel, *Ready Player One* (2011), was adapted into a movie directed by Steven Spielberg. The story takes place in 2045, in a future where virtual reality is used by the majority of the world. People escape the hardships of reality by entering the Oasis, the virtual realm in the story. There players can go on any imaginative adventure of their own making.

The movie was expected to have a positive effect on virtual reality sales. According to Jeremy Horwitz, writing on Venture Beat, HTC China president Alvin Wang Graylin revealed that a survey of Chinese customers indicated that there were signs that this was the case. As noted by Graylin, out of the 4,288 people who participated in the April 2018 survey, 60.3 percent of those who saw the movie planned on purchasing or upgrading a VR system in about a year. Out of those who did not see the movie, only 37.2 percent said they would do so.

Graylin said *Ready Player One* had a "significantly positive impact on intent for VR purchase in [the] next 12 months." China is proving to be the most promising country for VR adoption.

In the Real World

The film *Ready Player One*, based on a book of the same name, helped popularize virtual reality and was directed by Steven Spielberg.

VR Education

Maryland's Prince George's County Memorial Library System (PGCMLS) introduced VR to its patrons. With many teens in the system, PGCMLS wanted to engage young people in an exciting way. The Bowie library branch purchased an Oculus Rift to create meaningful programming. According to Mahnaz Dar, writing in the *School Library Journal*, the goal was for teens to "simulate multisensory experiences with virtual reality in order to invest new topics, construct meaning from new information, express

Virtual Reality and You

ideas, reflect on learning, and connect with others in and outside of their community."

There are a variety of VR experiences available at the Bowie library, according to Dar. These include virtual college campus tours, a visit to Syrian refugee camps, a tour of the White House led by the Obamas, and more. Library patrons were then able to create content of their own, such as movies and artwork, that can be viewed inside the headset.

Students and educators have numerous applications to choose from. *Boulevard* provides virtual access to art museums such as London's British Museum and New York City's Rubin Museum of Art. Students can interact with famous artworks while learning about each work's history. *InMind* takes students on a virtual tour of the human brain. Neurons fire all around the user in a short adventure

Two Royal British Legion members try the virtual reality experience of the Battle of Passchendaele at the Household Cavalry Museum in London, England.

In the Real World

game. Players search for neurons that cause mental disorders in this free VR game.

There are many more applications available that take students deep inside the pyramids, through outer space among the astronauts, or on a virtual stage to help overcome social anxiety and fear of public speaking. Many more are being developed to take advantage of the instructional potential of virtual reality.

Challenges

There are five major challenges facing VR companies today. The first is price. When the HTC Vive and Oculus Rift were first released, the prices were considered too high for anyone but early adopters and major virtual reality supporters. Lowering prices is not the answer for most VR manufacturers. If the prices are lowered too much, the companies cannot afford to produce the headsets. Without serious competition for VR hardware and demand from buyers, the prices are stagnant, waiting for technology to become cheaper with time.

The second big challenge is the lack of quality content for VR. There has not been a major game or piece of software that people have felt the overwhelming need to have in their homes.

Third, businesses have not yet figured out how to make selling VR a profitable pursuit. A business model is an operation of business that knows where to make profits, who the customers are, what product to make, and how to make it.

Another issue is the concern over the health effects of VR. Even if people are willing to tolerate some discomfort and motion sickness, there could be other physical, mental, or emotional effects they do not yet know about. Not enough research has been made either to identify or rule out health hazards. There is much left unknown about VR and **long-term** effects. Until more research is completed, people must experience VR at their own risk.

Finally, VR is still seen by many people as a gimmick. People will try it once, enjoy it, then have no desire to return to it. This situation

Virtual Reality and You

is particularly true for nongamers because most VR applications are geared for video game players. Businesses must find a way to show people the potential for VR experiences and how they can be worthwhile to users.

The Risk for Developers

Developers looking to break into virtual reality face a tough decision. They must invest their time and money into a new technology with no guarantees of success. Video game makers, for example, prefer to release their games for multiple platforms. Doing so allows them to sell their games to owners of HTC Vives, Oculus Rifts, and others. However, there are no set standards across the different VR platforms. Industry standards enable software to work across different platforms. Without standards, developers have to spend more time and money to get their software to work correctly on the different available headsets.

Nausea and headaches are common side effects of VR technology. Some people are able to tolerate the discomfort while others cannot.

In 2018, VR sales were lower than industry analysts predicted. One of the biggest factors was the lack of quality content. Microsoft even abandoned plans to bring VR to its popular Xbox video game console. According to Stefanie Fogel on Variety.com, Xbox's corporate vice president, Mike Ybarra, said in an interview with TechRadar that "there are still, in my opinion, challenges [in VR] to be solved." Augmented reality is the future for many companies. This possibility puts the future of VR, and for developers of VR content, on shaky ground.

CHAPTER 6

The Future

Despite the cloudy future of virtual reality, the technology continues to move forward. Technology challenges are addressed by those companies looking to move the industry forward.

More Than Games

Experiencing a VR environment is more than just playing video games. Companies and the health industry are finding new ways to integrate VR into their work. Theater chains and companies such as IMAX try to integrate virtual reality experiences into their business models.

Treating Anxiety Disorders

According to the Anxiety and Depression Association of America (ADAA), anxiety disorders are the most common mental illness in the United States. According to the ADAA's web page "Facts & Statistics," nearly forty million people who are eighteen years old or older are affected by anxiety conditions. Disorders include panic attacks, obsessive-compulsive disorder, and post-traumatic stress disorder. One way doctors treat patients with an anxiety disorder is by exposing them to whatever triggers their anxiety in a safe environment. For example, the anxiety could involve public speaking, social situations, or a fear of a specific object or situation, such as animals or heights.

Virtual Reality and You

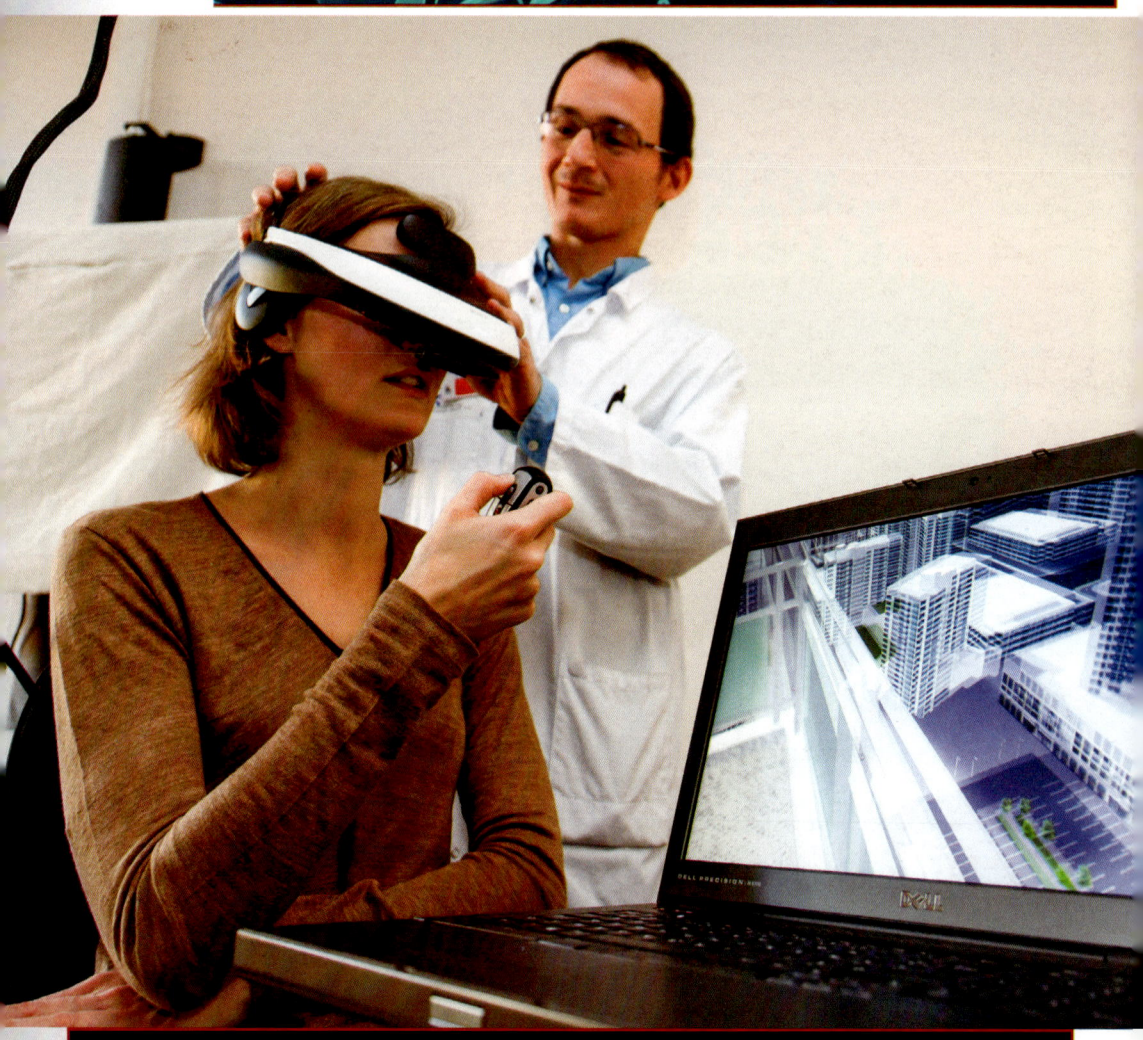

Researchers have discovered ways to apply virtual reality in medicine for treating people with acrophobia, or an extreme fear of heights.

    Researchers have found that VR is a great way to safely expose patients to their phobias. Patients can slowly learn to cope with their fears. For people with a fear of flying, VR can take them on a virtual flight. Studies show that those who have undertaken exposure

The Future

therapy for the fear of flying have significantly reduced their flight-related anxiety, as reported by Dr. Jessica L. Maples-Keller in the *Harvard Review of Psychiatry*. In one study, according to M. Rus-Calafell at the University of Barcelona in Spain, seven patients who were treated with VR therapy experienced less anxiety than those treated with imaginal exposure, where traumatic experiences are "re-lived" in a patient's thoughts and imagination. Four of the seven patients even took another flight after their VR therapy session. However, each individual is different, so the approach varies from person to person.

Physical Training

VR has proven to be a great way to get into good physical condition, too. There are many games that require players to move around. This option is a big change from traditional video games, where players sit in one place.

According to an online article on VR Fitness Insider, Bill Lindsay weighed 400 pounds (181 kilograms) by the time he invested in a VR system. He enjoyed being able to exercise at home, where his VR system was set up, versus having to go to a gym. Lindsay focused on improving his eating habits while using VR to workout for about an hour every other day. The games he played include BOXVR and Beat Saber. The games are designed so players move to a rhythm to achieve higher scores. For Lindsay, it also led to losing 90 pounds (41 kg) and improving his health.

For those with physical disabilities, VR represents an opportunity for new experiences. Maya Georgieva, digital learning director at The New School in New York City, was interviewed by Jeffrey R. Young on EdSurge in March 2018. Georgieva is aware of what the technology could do for many people. "I've had students who are completely unable to move, and we were able to actually put the

Virtual Reality and You

Virtual reality can help people with disabilities enjoy new experiences otherwise unavailable to them.

headset on them," she said, "and for them it was like a world of new opportunities because they're completely locked into a chair." Georgieva says that her campus is working on creating experiences for people with different disabilities.

Other Uses

Science students in college have found that getting time in a laboratory can be difficult. Google teamed up with a VR company called Labster to provide students with virtual labs to carry out their experiments. Inside their lab environments, students can view organisms in a microscope or sequence DNA. VR enables students to do things physically impossible, too, such as visit distant planets or manipulate time to speed up or slow down experiments. Several schools including Arizona State, the University of Texas at San Antonio, and MIT have adopted the virtual labs or plan to eventually.

VR helps businesses to build virtual prototypes of their products. By doing so, businesses can save time and money by avoiding real-world costs of building materials. Aircraft designers at Boeing and Airbus have taken advantage of VR technology. They are able to test new features, performance, and reliability in any type of condition they can create.

Virtual showrooms are another way businesses are integrating VR. These showrooms enable customers to try out products from the comfort of their own homes. People can test a new car, furniture,

The Future

Standalone Headsets

Untethered experiences are the next stage of VR. This stage means that people can move around freely without being physically connected to a computer. These new VR systems are called standalone. A variety of companies are attempting to set the standard for these standalones.

Facebook's Oculus Go is a $200 standalone headset. It is similar to the mobile phone-based Gear VR but without the need for a phone. Released in May 2018, the headset sold well, with 289,000 shipments made from May through July, as reported by Stefanie Fogel in *Variety*. The Lenovo Mirage Solo is a standalone headset made in conjunction with Google. Running the Daydream platform, it provides six degrees of freedom. However, the single controller is limited to 3DOF. Also launched in May 2018, it was initially available for $399.

Standalone headsets address one challenge of VR. However, these devices have yet to catch on with the mainstream buying public. This lack of popularity could be because the headsets are too expensive, not immersive enough, or there just is not enough compelling content available.

or other products virtually before making a purchase. In 2016, the Swedish furniture company IKEA introduced virtual showrooms that are available as an application for smartphones and the HTC Vive.

Privacy and Social Issues

There are companies looking into creating public spaces dedicated to VR. These are VR cafés, similar to the concept of internet cafés. The cafés provide VR access to their customers for a fee. They may cater to students, gamers, and event hosts. VR also offers social interactions between people hundreds of miles apart. There are various applications available that permit people to gather in virtual spaces.

However, there are moral concerns about privacy and keeping children safe within these social VR applications. Facebook has come under fire over concerns with people's personal data and information being kept private. Not only are people's information being kept by Facebook, that information is being sold to other companies without people's knowledge. These concerns have extended to their Oculus Rift and other VR headsets. VR facilitates a higher level of surveillance and data gathering.

For example, the company could track how users move and interact with virtual spaces. It could then guess how people are feeling one day based on their movements. Beyond that, private communications can be tracked, too. Data can be used to help fight users who send inappropriate messages or spam. However, Oculus has left the possibility of sharing personal data with other companies without users' knowledge open, as reported by Adi Robertson on The Verge website. These are some of the ethical dangers to privacy and consent that VR faces.

Oculus has introduced a Code of Conduct that lists what is and is not allowed for its users. This list includes a ban on sexually explicit, abusive, obscene, racially offensive, or illegal content. Social applications, however, must address conduct concerns within their own software. Without any safeguards, there is always the threat that underage VR users may be exposed to harmful behavior.

Some Ethical Issues

There are concerns about VR beyond those of user health and privacy. Ethical issues, or questions about what is morally right or wrong, involving VR include user isolation, desensitization, virtual crimes, and others. Companies such as Facebook already encounter questions about their use of people's private information. With VR headsets' ability to track a user's body movements as well as personal information, companies will have even greater access to consumers' private lives.

As Fiona J. McEvoy, a tech ethics researcher, points out on VentureBeat, users will have to be aware of how much time they are spending in the virtual world. Their time in VR could come at the expense of their real-world relationships, which suffer as users block out their surroundings behind headsets and headphones. In addition, playing a violent VR video game for too long could contribute to making someone less sensitive to actual violence. This effect of VR has already been used for positive results, such as desensitizing people with phobias like the fear of flying or public speaking, as already described. However, McEvoy reports that a US study showed that playing violent video games too often caused reduced sensitivity to emotions by users and a decrease in the ability to feel guilt among the study's participants. McEvoy also reports that some scientists have a very real concern that VR could be used by the military as a form of torture. Moreover, the line between virtual behavior and real-world crimes must be well defined to avoid the possible harmful effects of VR. The Virtual Reality Society, on its web page "Virtual Reality and Ethical Issues," says the issue is "whether it is possible for someone to suffer an injury or mental distress as a result of a violent action carried out in a virtual environment." Should VR "victims" be protected by the same laws that govern the real world?

Virtual reality presents an exciting world of possibilities. Many wonder if technology can ever create a truly immersive experience. Others wonder whether VR should be pursued at all.

Looking Ahead

The VR industry continues to improve on the technology of its products. Users of the first generation of headsets had to move their entire heads to interact with something. Soon, headsets will be able to track a user's eyes, allowing for even better immersion in VR. Brainwave technology will someday enable users to interact with

Virtual Reality and You

Children are vulnerable to inappropriate content and behavior while in a virtual world. Critics are concerned about the danger to personal data and information security that VR can pose.

virtual environments with only a thought, according to Bernard Marr, a contributor to *Forbes*.

In 2018, the VR industry was still searching for the one major application that makes it a must-have technology. It could come from an amazing game, new social tool, or an exciting way to interact with virtual environments. Virtual reality must also compete with augmented reality for mainstream adoption. In addition to smaller companies such as Magic Leap, Apple is forging ahead with that company's own tech. The barriers for VR—affordability, content, and technology advancement—are well known to those within the industry. Until they are addressed, people may either be on the doorstep of a new era of virtual worlds or waiting for technology to catch up with their dreams.

Glossary

anxiety disorder A mental condition in which people have intense, excessive, and persistent worry and fear about everyday situations.

augmented reality Technology that places or lays computer-generated images on a user's view of the world around them.

business model How a business plans on making a profit.

cognitive Relating to conscious mental activities including thinking, reasoning, remembering, imagining, learning words, and using language.

component A part of a machine or system.

feedback The return to the input of a part of the output of a system.

immersive Providing deep involvement in something such as an artificial environment.

inside-out tracking Movement tracking in VR done without markers around the environment.

multisensory Involving more than one sense.

nausea A condition of the stomach when a person feels like vomiting.

neurological In relation to a person's nerves and the nervous system.

ophthalmology A branch of medical science dealing with the structure, functions, and diseases of the eye.

Virtual Reality and You

platform The computer hardware and components using a particular operating system.

real-time When computer data is processed almost immediately.

screen-door effect When visible fine lines between pixels on a display make viewing a display feel like looking out of a screen door.

spam Irrelevant or inappropriate messages sent on the internet or through VR.

standalone In VR, the ability to operate without the need of other hardware or software.

stationary Fixed in a position.

surveillance A careful watch or observation of something.

virtual reality An artificial environment that is experienced through sights and sounds provided by a computer and in which one's actions partly decide what happens in the environment.

For More Information

EdCan Network

60 St. Clair Avenue East, Suite 703
Toronto, ON M4T 1N5
Canada
(416) 591-6300
Website: https://www.edcan.ca
Facebook: @cea.ace
Twitter: @EdCanNet
YouTube: @CdnEducAssn
For more than 125 years, the EdCan Network has supported teachers and students in reaching their potential. The organization provides information on VR learning, as well as other tech tools for the classroom.

Global Virtual Reality Association

Email: info@gvra.com
Website: https://www.gvra.com
Facebook: @GlobalVRAssociation
The Global Virtual Reality Association, founded by Google, Samsung Group, and the Sony Corporation, is a nonprofit organization interested in developing virtual reality and establishing best practices among companies.

Virtual Reality Society (VRS)

Website: https://www.vrs.org.uk
Facebook: @VirtualRealitySociety
Virtual Reality Society provides news, information, and education about virtual reality and the challenges it faces.

Virtual Reality and You

The VR/AR Association

Email: info@thevrara.com
Website: http://www.thevrara.com
Facebook: @vrarassociation
Twitter: @thevrara
The VR/AR Association helps bring companies together to collaborate on VR and AR projects and educate member organizations and companies.

Web3D Consortium

650 Castro Street, Suite #120–490
Mountain View, CA 94041
(248) 342-7662
Website: http://www.web3d.org
Facebook: @Web3D-Consortium
Twitter: @Web3Dconsortium
The Web3D Consortium is an international nonprofit organization. It supports the development of interactive 3D graphics including virtual reality technology.

For Further Reading

Allen, John. *Improving Virtual Reality*. San Diego, CA: ReferencePoint Press, 2018.

Centore, Michael. *Entertainment Industry* (STEM in Current Events). Broomall, PA: Mason Crest, 2017.

Challoner, Jack, Ben Kidd, and Ed Barton. *Virtual Reality*. New York, NY: DK Publishing, 2017.

Cline, Ernest. *Ready Player One*. New York, NY: Random House Audio, 2018.

Gregory, Josh. *Careers in Virtual Reality Technology*. Ann Arbor, MI: Cherry Lake Publishing, 2019.

Henneberg, Susan, ed. *Virtual Reality* (Opposing Viewpoints). New York, NY: Greenhaven Publishing, 2017.

Kallen, Stuart A. *Cutting Edge Entertainment Technology*. San Diego, CA: ReferencePoint Press, 2017.

Martin, Brett S. *Virtual Reality*. Chicago, IL: Norwood House Press, 2018.

Mooney, Carla. *What Is the Future of Virtual Reality?* San Diego, CA: ReferencePoint Press, 2017.

Peterson, Christy. *Cutting-edge Virtual Reality* (Spotlight Books). Minneapolis, MN: Lerner Publications, 2019.

Rauf, Don. *Virtual Reality* (Digital and Information Literacy). New York, NY: Rosen Publishing, 2016.

Bibliography

Anxiety and Depression Association of America, ADAA. "Facts & Statistics." Retrieved September 24, 2018. https://adaa.org.

Ashworth, James, Ally Leigh, Sophie Von Der Tann, Conor Hamilton, Grace Davis, Adithi Shenava, Connor Thirlwell, and Sophie Kilminster. "Oxford Scientists Produce VR Psychological Therapist—The Oxford Student." The Oxford Student, August 9, 2018. https://www.oxfordstudent.com.

Belman, Laurel. "Success Born of Failure: The Nintendo Power Glove." Invention | Lemelson Center for the Study of Invention and Innovation, July 23, 2015. http://invention.si.edu/success-born-failurenintendo-power-glove.

Betters, Elyse. "Virtual Reality: Lessons from the Past for Oculus Rift." BBC News, August 30, 2013. https://www.bbc.com.

Chafkin, Max, and Annie Leibovitz. "Why Facebook's $2 Billion Bet on Oculus Rift Might One Day Connect Everyone on Earth." The Hive, November 30, 2017. https://www.vanityfair.com.

Comen, Evan. "How Much Did a Personal Computer Cost the Year You Were Born?" *USA Today*, June 22, 2018. https://www.usatoday.com/story/tech/2018/06/22/cost-of-a-computer-the-year-you-wereborn/36156373.

Computer History Museum. "1965: Mainframe Computers Employ ICs." The Silicon Engine. Retrieved September 24, 2018. http://www.computerhistory.org/siliconengine/mainframe-computers-employ-ics.

Dar, Mahnaz. "3 Steps for Introducing Teens to Virtual Reality | ALA Midwinter 2018." *School Library Journal*, February 21, 2018. https://www.slj.com/?detailStory=3-steps-introducing-teens-virtual-reality-ala-midwinter2018.

Bibliography

Deahl, Dani. "Google Is Making It Easier to Create 3D Audio for VR." The Verge, November 7, 2017. https://www.theverge.com/2017/11/6/16614348/google-resonance-audio-3d-sound-vr-ar.

Dingman, Hayden. "Microsoft Windows Mixed Reality Review: Easy to Set Up, Hard to Use." *PCWorld*, May 11, 2018. https://www.pcworld.com/article/3269791/virtual-reality/windows-mixed-reality-review-steamvr.html.

Dredge, Stuart. "The Complete Guide to Virtual Reality—Everything You Need to Get Started." *Guardian*, November 10, 2016. https://www.theguardian.com/technology/2016/nov/10/virtual-reality-guideheadsets-apps-games-vr.

Earnshaw, Rae A., Huw Jones, and Michael Gigante. *Virtual Reality Systems*. Tokyo, Japan: Academic Press, 1994.

Edwards, Benj. "The Wacky World of VR in the 80s and 90s." *PC Magazine*, April 27, 2018. https://www.pcmag.com/feature/343351/the-wacky-world-of-vr-in-the-80s-and-90s.

Feltham, Jamie, and Upload VR. "The Elder Scrolls V: Skyrim Tops List of PSVR's Most-played Games in U.S." VentureBeat, August 17, 2018. https://venturebeat.com/2018/08/18/the-elder-scrolls-v-skyrim-top-list-of-psvrs-most-played-games-in-u-s.

Fogel, Stefanie. "Despite Strong Oculus Go Sales, VR Fever Is Cooling (Analyst)." *Variety*, July 27, 2018. https://variety.com/2018/gaming/hardware/superdata-vr-sales-report-1202878145.

Greenwald, Will. "Top 10 Most Influential Tech Advances of the Decade." *PC Magazine*, January 4, 2011. https://www.pcmag.com/article2/0,2817,2374825,00.asp.

Virtual Reality and You

Gurman, Mark. "Spielberg's 'Ready Player One' Lends VR Timely Marketing Boost." Bloomberg.com, March 26, 2018. https://www.bloomberg.com.

Hignett, Katherine. "Witnessing Devastation in Hiroshima: Survivors Retell Their Stories 73 Years after the Atomic Bomb Dropped." *Newsweek*, August 6, 2018. https://www.newsweek.com/remembering-hiroshima-73-years-after-bomb-1056615.

Hoalst, Shane. "Bill Loses 90 Pounds with Beat Saber, BOXVR, Weights and Healthy Eating!" VR Fitness Insider, August 21, 2018. https://www.vrfitnessinsider.com.

Holt, Kris. "Google's Daydream Science Labs Bring STEM Experiments to VR." Engadget, August 23, 2018. https://www.engadget.com/2018/08/23/google-labster-vr-science-labs-daydream-stem-students.

Horwitz, Jeremy. "HTC: Ready Player One Boosted VR Buying Interest by 23% in China." VentureBeat, May 17, 2018. https://venturebeat.com.

LaMotte, Sandee. "The Very Real Health Dangers of Virtual Reality." CNN, December 13, 2017. https://www.cnn.com/2017/12/13/health/virtual-reality-vr-dangers-safety/index.html.

Lardinois, Frederic. "The Story Behind Google's Cardboard Project." TechCrunch. June 26, 2014. https://techcrunch.com.

Lomas, Natasha. "This VR Cycle Is Dead." TechCrunch, August 26, 2017. https://techcrunch.com/2017/08/26/this-vr-cycle-is-dead.

Lynch, Matthew. "20 of the Best Virtual Reality Games in Education." The Edvocate, May 22, 2017. https://www.theedadvocate.org.

Bibliography

Maples-Keller, Jessica L., Brian E. Bunnell, Sae-Jin Kim, and Barbara O. Rothbaum. "The Use of Virtual Reality Technology in the Treatment of Anxiety and Other Psychiatric Disorders." *Harvard Review of Psychiatry* 25, no. 3 (May–June 2017): 103–13. https://www.ncbi.nlm.nih.gov/pmc/articles/PMC5421394.

Marr, Bernard. "The Amazing Ways Companies Use Virtual Reality for Business Success." *Forbes*, July 31, 2017. https://www.forbes.com.

Matney, Lucas. "Oculus Implements Its Own GDPR-compliant Privacy Controls." TechCrunch, April 19, 2018. https://techcrunch.com.

McEvoy, Fiona J. "10 Ethical Concerns That Will Shape the VR Industry." VentureBeat, January 5, 2018. https://venturebeat.com/2018/01/04/10-ethical-concerns-that-will-shape-the-vr-industry.

McKie, Robin. "Virtual Reality Headsets Could Put Children's Health at Risk." *Guardian*, October 28, 2017. https://www.theguardian.com/technology/2017/oct/28/virtual-reality-headset-children-cognitive-problems.

Mealy, Paul. *Virtual & Augmented Reality*. Hoboken, NJ: John Wiley & Sons, 2018.

Mukamal, Reena. "Are Virtual Reality Headsets Safe for Eyes?" American Academy of Ophthalmology, April 12, 2017. https://www.aao.org/eye-health/tips-prevention/arevirtual-reality-headsets-safe-eyes.

Nuga, Haruka. "Japanese Students Recreate Hiroshima Bombing in VR." *Time*, August 6, 2018. http://time.com/5358430/japan-virtual-reality-hiroshima.

Paton, Callum. "A Virtual Reality Gamer Has Died from Blood Loss after Slipping." *Newsweek*, December 23, 2017. https://www.newsweek.com.

Pierce, David. "The Inside Story of Google's Daydream, Where VR Feels Like Home." *Wired*, June 3, 2017. https://www.wired.com/2017/01/google-daydream-vr-feels-human.

Pino, Nick. "HTC Vive Review." TechRadar, July 23, 2018. https://www.techradar.com/reviews/wearables/htc-vive-1286775/review.

Pino, Nick. "Oculus Rift Review." TechRadar, July 23, 2018. https://www.techradar.com/reviews/gaming/gaming-accessories/oculus-rift-1123963/review.

Pino, Nick. "PlayStation VR Review." TechRadar, August 11, 2018. https://www.techradar.com/reviews/gaming/playstation-vr-1235379/review.

Robertson, Adi. "Facebook Data Concerns Spread to Oculus and VR." The Verge, April 9, 2018. https://www.theverge.com/2018/4/9/17206650/oculus-facebook-vr-user-data-mining-privacy-policy-advertising.

Rus-Calafell, Mar, José Gutiérrez-Maldonado, Cristina Botella, and Rosa M. Baños. "Virtual Reality Exposure and Imaginal Exposure in the Treatment of Fear of Flying." *Behavior Modification* Volume 37, no. 4 (July 2014): 568–90. https://www.ncbi.nlm.nih.gov/pubmed/23585557.

Samit, Jay. "A Possible Cure for Virtual Reality Motion Sickness." *Fortune*, February 6, 2018. http://fortune.com/2018/02/06/virtual-reality-motion-sickness.

Sankin, Aaron. "The Virtual Reality Gaming Revolution That Wasn't." The Kernel, June 28, 2015. https://kernelmag

Bibliography

.dailydot.com/issue-sections/features-issue-sections/13516/virtuality-return-of-virtual-reality.

Slavova, Yoana, and Mu Mu. "A Comparative Study of the Learning Outcomes and Experience of VR in Education." In *IEEE Conference on Virtual Reality and 3D User Interfaces (IEEE VR 2018)*. Retrieved August 29, 2018. http://www.northampton.ac.uk/wp-content/uploads/2018/04/Virtual-Reality-overview.pdf.

Souppouris, Aaron. "How HTC and Valve Built the Vive." Engadget, March 8, 2016. https://www.engadget.com/2016/03/18/htc-vive-an-oral-history.

Stein, Scott. "The Real Danger of Virtual Reality." CNET, March 29, 2016. https://www.cnet.com/news/the-dangers-of-virtual-reality.

Ternovyi, Dmytro. "7 Ways to Start a VR Café." VentureBeat, February 10, 2018. https://venturebeat.com.

Virtual Reality Society. "Virtual Reality and Ethical Issues." Retrieved September 25, 2018. https://www.vrs.org.uk.

Williams, Brian, and Kerry Sanders. "Virtual Reality and Simulator Sickness." Report on NBC's *Focus*, aired June 29, 1996. YouTube video, 4:01. Posted by "VRtifacts," December 15, 2009. https://www.youtube.com/watch?time_continue=1&v=O0arluK5zrQ&ab_channel=VRtifacts.

Wolwort, Kate. "5 Major Challenges for the VR Industry | Articles | Chief Technology Officer." Innovation Enterprise, March 23, 2018. https://channels.theinnovationenterprise.com/articles/5-major-challenges-of-vr-industry.

Young, Jeffrey R. "VR Could Bring a New Era of Immersive Learning. But Ethical and Technical Challenges Remain." EdSurge, March 20, 2018. https://www.edsurge.com.

Index

A
advances in technology, 30–31
anxiety disorders, 43–45
applications, 9, 11, 12–13, 17, 18, 32, 36, 40, 41, 42, 47–48, 50
augmented reality, 13–14, 38, 42, 50

B
brainwave technology, 49–50

C
challenges, 24, 27, 36, 37, 41–42, 43, 47
Code of Conduct, 48
computer-generated images, 14
computer revolution, 22
Consumer Electronics Show, 37

D
dangers, 15–21
  cognitive issues, 20–21
  example of, 17
  nausea, 17–19
  tangled up, 15–17
  too close, 19
data gathering, 48
degrees of freedom, 9, 32, 33, 47
desensitization, 48, 49

E
ethical issues, 48–49

F
flight simulator, 24

G
goggles, 4, 17, 22

H
headset, 7, 8, 9, 11, 13, 14, 15, 16, 17, 19, 21, 22, 27, 28, 31, 32, 33, 34, 36, 37, 38, 40, 41, 42, 46, 47, 48, 49
health industry, 43
HTC Vive, 18, 32–34, 41, 42, 47

I
immersion, 9, 11, 15, 29, 49
immersive experience, 7, 9, 13, 27, 34, 36, 47, 49
inside-out tracking, 9, 34

M
Microsoft, 34, 37, 42
Moore's Law, 28, 29
moral concerns, 48
more than games, 43

Index

O
Oculus Rift, 18, 31–32, 33, 39, 41, 42, 48
other uses, 46–47

P
physical training, 45–46
PlayStation VR, 36
Power Glove, 25–27, 28
privacy issues, 47

R
Ready Player One, 38
risk for developers, 42

S
screen-door effect, 34
shaky business, 37
simulated environment, 4, 13
simulated motion, 18
social issues, 47
standalone headsets, 15, 47

T
therapy, 6, 13, 45

V
video games, 25, 27, 28, 32, 36, 42, 43, 45, 49
Virtual Boy, 28

Virtuality, 27
virtual reality (VR), 4
  additions to, 11
  benefits of, 12–13
  concerns, 20, 28–29, 41, 48, 49
  critics of, 6, 15
  in education, 13, 38, 39
  experiencing history with, 6
  future of, 43–50
  health effects of, 21, 41
  history of, 22–24
  looking ahead, 49
  meaning of, 7–11
  parts of, 7–8
  in real world, 37–42
  types of, 9
virtual reality revolution, 34, 36
Virtual Reality Society, 49
Virtual Visual Environment Display (VIVED), 24
VR death, 17, 33–34
VR education, 39–41
VR industry, 37, 38, 49, 50
VR therapy, 6, 45

W
wireless controllers, 11
wireless solutions, 15
witnessing history, 4–6

About the Author

Jeff Mapua is the author of technology-focused books including *A Career in Customer Service and Tech Support*, *Net Neutrality and What It Means to You*, *A Career as a Social Media Manager*, *Respecting Digital Content*, and *Programming*. From the NES Power Glove to the Google Daydream, Mapua has been an avid VR fan for many years. He lives in Batavia, Illinois, with his wife, Ruby.

Photo Credits

Cover (man with VR glasses) franz12/Shutterstock.com; pp. 4–5 © AP Images; p. 8 franckreporter/E+/Getty Images; pp. 10–11 g-stockstudio/Shutterstock.com; pp. 12–13 Boris Horvat/AFP/Getty Images; p. 16 Ruby Porter/The Image Bank/Getty Images; p. 18 Agnieszka Olek/Caiaimage/Getty Images; pp. 20–21 Thomas Barwick/DigitalVision/Getty Images; p. 23 NASA; p. 26 Piero Cruciatti/Alamy Stock Photo; p. 28 Maurice Savage/Alamy Stock Photo; p. 31 Allen J. Schaben/Los Angeles Times/Getty Images; pp. 33, 34–35 Bloomberg/Getty Images; p. 39 Lifestyle pictures/Alamy Stock Photo; p. 40 Daniel Leal-Olivas/AFP/Getty Images; p. 42 Andrey_Popov/Shutterstock.com; pp. 44–45 Phanie/Alamy Stock Photo; p. 46 marino bocelli/Shutterstock.com; p. 50 izusek/E+/Getty Images; cover (top) and interior pages background (circuit board) jijomathai/Shutterstock.com; additional interior pages circuit board image gandroni/Shutterstock.com.

Design/Layout: Brian Garvey; Senior Editor: Kathy Kuhtz Campbell; Photo Researcher: Karen Huang